PERSEVERANCE

The Story of Mary Jane Patterson

By: Quineka Ragsdale

Melanin Origins

Published by Melanin Origins LLC
PO Box 122123; Arlington, TX 76012
Copyright 2018

First Edition
The author asserts the moral right under the Copyright, Designs and Patents Act of 1988 to be
identified as the author of this work.

Library of Congress Control Number: 2018938047

ISBN: 978-1-62676-780-5 hardback
ISBN: 978-1-62676-788-1 paperback
ISBN: 978-1-62676-787-4 ebook

Dedication

This work is dedicated to children everywhere who have lost hope in today's education system. One thing is true about learning, and this will follow you throughout your own life – no one can take your skills away from you. You were born with the innate ability to impact change in this world AND you can do anything that you put your mind to, BUT your skills must be cultivated (ask your parents what "cultivated" means). This is why education is important. In order to be the best person that you want to be and in order to experience all of the fun that you wish to have in life – you must take learning seriously. We hope this story encourages you to shoot for the stars and beyond.

--Louie T. McClain II
Founder/CEO
Melanin Origins LLC

Sometimes it's hard to believe in yourself, but you can do anything you put your mind to.

I am sure of this because things weren't always easy for me; but through perseverance, I was able to accomplish some amazing things!

My name is Mary Jane Patterson. I was once just a small girl from a big family in North Carolina.

My dad was a brick maker and my mom spent most of her day teaching my siblings and I.

My parents wanted my siblings and I to get a very good education, so we packed up and moved to Oberlin, Ohio.

There were so many fun people in our community. We all worked hard to help each other out and keep each other encouraged.

My parents even let other students live with us so they could have an opportunity go to school.

A lot of people chose not to go to college, but my sister and I really wanted to go. We wanted to learn as much as we could so we could help other people.

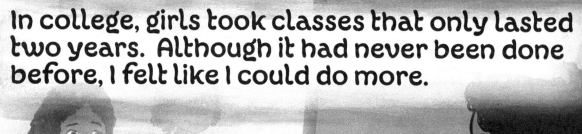

In college, girls took classes that only lasted two years. Although it had never been done before, I felt like I could do more.

I really had to believe in myself to do something that no one else had ever done.

It took a while, but through perseverance, I finally did it! I was the first African American woman to earn a four-year Bachelor's degree.

I was able to reach my goal because I never gave up! I believed that just because no one else had done it before did not mean that I couldn't do it.

After reaching my goal, I wanted to do more. I left Ohio and moved to Philadelphia, Pennsylvania to be a teacher.

I wanted to teach the kids in Philadelphia to believe in themselves and dream big just like I did.

After I helped kids in Philadelphia, I moved to Washington D.C.; I wanted make a difference in the lives of those kids too.

The school leaders noticed the impact I was having on the kids, and they decided to make me the principal of the entire school!

Being the principal helped me to inspire all the kids in the school.

Now that I'm finished helping them, I want to help you in the same way.

If you have a goal that you really want to reach, keep working at it. Persevere and never give up!

One day you will reach your goals and then you can help others reach theirs as well.

CPSIA information can be obtained
at www.ICGtesting.com
Printed in the USA
LVHW061214290819
629185LV00001B/10/P

9 781626 767881